STARING AT A HOOPOE

David Cooke

For Veronica
with best wishes
David

19th May 2022

Staring at a Hoopoe

© David Cooke

First Edition 2020
ISBN: 978-1-913329-08-2

David Cooke has asserted his authorship and given his permission to
Dempsey & Windle for these poems to be published here.

Frontispiece:'Staring at a Hoopoe' ©2020 Janice Dempsey
based on a photograph of Eugenio Montale

Published by Dempsey & Windle
15 Rosetrees
Guildford
Surrey
GU1 2HS
UK
01483 571164
dempseyandwindle.com

British Library Cataloguing-in-Publication Data
A catalogue record for this book is available from the British Library

By the Same Author

Brueghel's Dancers
In the Distance
Work Horses
A Slow Blues: Poems 1972-2012
A Murmuration
After Hours
Reel to Reel

Livet forstås baglæns, men må leves forlæns

Life is understood backwards, but has to be lived forwards

Søren Kierkegaard

CONTENTS

FEELING THE FEAR

You ask for advice but what can I say?
Piranhas teem in the quietest streams.
So feel the fear and do it anyway.

You might have blazed above the dismal fray,
if only the stars had sanctioned your schemes.
You ask for advice but what can I say?

No one who knows you can sense your dismay.
A residual issue wrecks your dreams.
So feel the fear and do it anyway.

Bullet points, mantras, and thoughts for the day
won't fix what's falling apart at the seams.
You ask for advice but what can I say?

Lacking the confidence others display,
you sense darkness creeping beyond what seems
to be. Feel the fear, but do it anyway.

For none can tell you the forces at play
when the admonitory hoopoe screams.
You ask my advice but what can I say?
Just feel the fear and do it anyway.

THE MAGUS

It's as if his powers were not enough,
when he feels such a need to engage you
and speaks with his hangdog look of the streets
he came from and the doubts that wore him down,
making him seem much less than you or me,
were it not for the hand of one who saved him.

Out in the world on his own, he turns it
upside down and, like a man who is cadging
his bus fare home, will ask for a coin
that melts away, then somehow reappears
in the can of coke you nearly opened,
until distracted momentarily.

Your time, your money, are nothing to him,
illusions he'll change with a casual
glance. Why fret to save the appearances?
The hands of your watch spin out of control.
Just as easily they'll stop forever.
He can scatter dollars like random leaves.

Who was it told you how everything flows,
that tables and chairs are clouds of atoms,
that glass is merely an icy river?
When he reaches through its sluggish currents
he finds what you desire: the dazzle of jewels
and metal, however cheap or overprized.

Such things are merely tokens in the games
he plays. He sees through them as he has seen
through you, spelling out your secret thought
on a distant hoarding or filling up
a room with the warmth of a memory,
released in a whisper of butterflies' wings.

CAPTAIN WEBB

I remember his name and features
from my brief matchbox phase
that sparked up and fizzled out
like so many others. *Phillumeny*,
yes, that's the word. Cutting out the labels,
I glued them to homemade charts.

When Bryant and May raised his profile,
he couldn't have been more famous
if he had stared from banknotes.
On a cheap box of lucifers
– the white cliffs at his back –
his pose is muscular, relaxed.

In an age when maps were
splotched in red and folding stuff
was no concern of any working man,
he seemed such a *British* hero,
the first one to swim the moat
that maintains *la différence*.

And sensing that achievement
ends up as commonplace
he moved on to stunts that paid
– like a man surprising you
by what he'll do for bets – aware
that easy money soon evaporates.

Afloat in a tank for days on end,
watching clouds, did he see the future –
minor celebrities desperate
'to give something back' or even you
and me, greased up for charity,
ticking off our bucket list?

His style was never flashy.
Dour and dogged wins the race.
Burnt out and broke, his final plunge
was madness. Spat out by rapids
beneath Niagara Falls, his plot
in Oakwood is called 'The Stranger's Rest'.

SWALLOW

Her slow ascent
to the platform
effaces time –
her flexing
grip on the rail,
the soft pad
of her step.
Reaching the edge
of the board,
she hesitates,
absorbing
its spring.
Heels raised,
arms stretched,
she senses
that this
is all that
she can know
of flight.
Her gaze
uplifted,
her back arched
taut as a bow,
she breasts
the air,
craving its pull –
a shift
in the elements
that may one day
release her.

SWIMMER

Each time he slips beneath the surface
he senses everything falling away.
All that's left is movement,
the stretch and reach of muscle
– his lungs pumped, his diaphragm
like a tightened strap.

Parting the water, he leaves
no trace beyond a brief ripple,
pursuing his path, stroke
by stroke, until he rises for air.
Deafened by its din, he is blinded
by plate-glass windows.

Returning to his element,
he will pit himself against himself
for as long as it takes
for him to feel he's ready –
his weekly tally increasing,
his technique seamless.

He will set the scene where
he chooses: a quiet cove or a lakeside,
lucent with meaning. There is only
distance now between him
and the point he dreams of,
where endurance ceases.

MINGUS

Never willing
to accept his place
or stroke
the violoncello politely
for a bow-tied
maestro,
only the bass
could match
his ego.
Swaying, possessed,
like a holy roller,
he goaded
his band,
and slapped
the strings
to imprecation,
whoop
and holler.

HORACE SILVER

Feeling no urge
to ransack harmony
or play more notes
when a few were enough
– burnished
and buoyant
as waves that wash
the Cape Verde Islands –
he hunched down
over the keys
and dug in deep
until, at last,
he made out
his old man's features,
smiling back
contentedly,
and smoking, as ever,
his rank cheroot.

SOUL
for Grant Tarbard

Northern kids, their futures
predictable, they grafted dourly
five days a week down pits, in shops
and on the factory floor –
paying their way with some left
for vinyl, speed and threads.

Travelling miles by train each
weekend with a change of clothes
and a box of classic tracks
– minor hits and rarities
by blacks the charts ignored –
they kept the faith

and stormed the bouncers
– who lost their cool and didn't get it –
once doors were opened
to another drenched all-nighter
at Wigan Casino, the Highland Room,
the Golden Torch, the Wheel.

A four-four beat was all
they needed, rock steady,
relentless, and simple lyrics
that told the truth. Hallucogenics
and hopeless solos
warped the walls of bedsits

in never-never land,
but lads in bags and polo shirts,
their girls in swirling skirts,
danced all night till morning.
Doing splits and fancy tricks,
they span around like dervishes.

SPEECHLESS

When he hears us calling
his name he knows
it's him we mean –
its tongue-tap, resonance,
and murmur of labials ...
Yet now he is making
himself at home,
our expectations wither.
We wait for a hint, a trickle ...

He can shape a word
with his hands, or share
his madcap smile.
He can reach out
and grab his brother's
favourite car –
when 'Mine! No! Mine!'
fills his ears
with its shrill refusal.

Mopping up frustration,
his mother sweeps him
into her arms and says
his name again.
It lets him know
he's *perfect,*
whole, complete ...

Like her we hold
our breath. Like him
we hold our peace.

FOR JEFFREY HUDSON
(1619 – 1682)

The lonely queen's poppet, her living toy,
he was no more than eighteen inches tall
the day he burst through the crust of a pie:
the model of manners making the man,
his step as sturdy as a cavalier's.

In a childish age he seemed a wonder,
the butcher's boy from Oakham, whose father,
a brawny-shouldered rogue, supplied the beasts
for baiting rings, his wily lad stepping
featly to the scrape of a country jig.

At least the child had made his way, his wits
above the average and blessed by what
he lacked, when a duke – who had turned his hand
to nothing beyond court masque and intrigue –
allowed him his chance to hog the limelight.

Yet how much darker the shadow he casts
than that of a fop or the popinjay
he shot for a slight to his self-esteem
among the performing fools and monkeys,
the sights you'd see in a travelling show.

His one act of recklessness annulling
the life he'd gained, he was exiled, enslaved,
then ransomed decades later. All he left
behind were bones, his name, and one receipt
he had signed in his tired, wavering hand.

STARING AT A HOOPOE

ilare uccello calunniato
   Eugenio Montale

Caught in the moment,
there is no way of knowing
who might have blinked first –
the old man or his visitant,
the bright, crested
ambivalent bird. A few
scattered objects
implying a workspace,
the room is otherwise
unfocused beyond
the reciprocal stare
of two survivors.
The eyes of one are stoical,
but lit by a sense
that all is not determined.
The other's are steeled,
impenetrable – the maligned
harbinger of spring
or a bird whose piping
mnemonic call
is like a final summons.

THE WAY ART PEPPER TELLS IT

In San Quentin prison the psychos,
thieves and junkies exchange
desolate tales, and each one's
a variation on a theme
that ends the same. Breathing in
and breathing out
to keep his panic at bay,
the man with the sax
is no exception when he tells his
in a different way.
Reinventing where he's been,
one shimmering note
at a time, the way ahead's unclear.
Stuck with the changes,
he plays them
the way he feels today.

IN PÈRE LACHAISE CEMETERY

It takes time and focus to make your way
around this star-studded necropolis.
Without a convenient map or a guide
– pedantic, wry, and always affable –
you'll wander in vain its endless pathways.
Unable to spot the names you've heard of,
you will feel deceived and none the wiser.

Lured by the bones and dubious remains
of two mythic lovers, what do we seek
before a monument built long after
their passion was spent? For who now recalls
the scholar and the edifice he built;
or the bright girl who honed his thought
but had to share in his calamities?

No eloquent poet, no dead master,
rises up between the trees to greet you
and lead you around in ordered circles
where penalties always mirror the crime.
The sins of some here are known, indulged now
by a different age with different values –
whose adulation sees beyond their flaws.

Whatever they drank, smoked, or may have pumped
into their world-weary veins, it matters
little now to the fans who love their work,
however they cheated or got their kicks.
Though sectioned off for his own protection,
The Lizard King lies in state, accepting
tributes: the chewing gum stuck to his tree.

The Sparrow's voice still resonates beyond
each tragic circumstance, her bourgeois slab
supplied by one who, those years she suffered,
had no gift that healed her. Abandoning
his wit, the martyred poet and author
of a play called *Salomé* lies at last
with his love and lipsticked flocks of kisses.

MY FORMER LIFE
Baudelaire

For years I dwelled in a lofty palace
that sun and sea suffused with blazing light;
whose pillars towering above their site
seemed each evening a cavern of basalt.

The ocean refracted shimmering skies
and reattuned their perfect harmony,
rich and solemn, to the visionary
tints of twilight reflected in my eyes.

And there I wallowed in self-indulgence,
lapped by soothing water, each day a blur,
as I gazed on barely clad retainers.

Fanning my brow with palms, their unguents
exquisite, they were tasked to embellish
ennui, my unaccountable anguish.

LOCKS

Along the Pont des Arts the lovers
plight their troth with padlocks.
Engraved with names and blazoned
with bright painted hearts,
they attach them optimistically,
then throw away the key.
Tokens offered to the gods of love,
they have spread like ivy,
so are now deemed an eyesore
by the powers that be.

TRUST
for Bernadette

The summer sales are in full swing.
For what it's worth I've tagged along,
trailing behind you through a maze
of bright concessions: *Kaliko,
Diesel, Coast*, and then on past *Dash* ...

My take on colour imprecise,
my sense of the fashionable
shaky, I suggest, when pushed,
the dresses I think will suit you,
then wait for you to try them on.

Abiding my summons, I grab
a chair – the sales assistant's smile
indulgent – until I'm absorbed
in random thoughts that dissipate
once I'm drawn towards two figures.

What is it about them that seems
unsettling? Identical, too,
I note with a start. Sisters, then,
and middle-aged, joined by a third
who is soon all flap and fluster.

Left alone momentarily
by a rail of bargains too good
to ignore, they stare like two blank
mirrors into the other's gaze –
clasping their hands as if at prayer.

Nothing stirs their self-composure.
here where each display's strategic
and logos catch the eye – as you
now return to mine in a blaze
of yellow well worth the gamble.

CHASIN' THE TRANE

Each night he plays
the Vanguard
you'll hear him
stretching solos
for an hour
at a time –
till all he needs
is Elvin
stoking the drums
while Tyner
and the bassist
sit it out
at the bar,
wondering when,
if ever,
they'll hear
him reprising
a recognizable
theme.

SONNY

Praised to the skies
by a musicologist
when all
he had done
was play the blues,
he took time off
to clear his head.
Without
a padded loft
or a tumbledown
woodshed
in the Lower
East Side
of crowded
Manhattan,
he blew his sax
come rain or shine
way up on the Bridge.

FOUND

You could start off with the memoirs of one
long dead and preferably eccentric –
an eighteenth century non-conformist,
or one of the first lepidopterists,
who might be a prince, explorer, or cad,
his eyes on stalks for a telling detail.

Cut and paste correspondence, retaining
orthographic quirks, the dialectal
buzz and burr of a self-taught radical,
as faithful to his vision as you are
now to his words. Invent or change nothing.
Your tricks will undermine the text's true worth.

And since 'description is revelation'
– as Wallace Stevens said, who spent his life
responding to balance sheets and memos –
you could do much worse than Observers' books,
manuals, the mediaeval travellers'
tales of oriental, despotic courts.

The world is filled with things. It is today
and ever was, with specialists at hand,
who will spell out each quiddity for you.
Time is a mystery, but clocks tick tock
precisely. Clunking, homely, ornamental –
there's always an object to fit the slot.

WHISPER IN AGONY
Jules Supervielle

Don't be surprised,
but close your eyes
till they become
opaque as stone.

And let the heart be,
for should it stop
it flutters still
on its secret slope.

Your hands will lie
at rest beside you
in their barge of ice,

your forehead bare
as the empty space
dividing armies.

FROM MIDDLESBROUGH TO MOSEL
i.m. Gertrude Bell (1868 – 1926)

Gertrude Margaret Lowthian Bell (14 July 1868 – 12 July 1926) was, amongst many other things, a traveller, archaeologist, linguist and cartographer. Born into an industrial family in the North of England, she was one of the first women to be educated at Oxford University and was awarded the best history degree in her year. She later played a significant role in Middle Eastern politics because of the knowledge and contacts she had built up in the course of her travels across Syria, Mesopotamia, Asia Minor, and Arabia. Along with T.E. Lawrence, she helped support the Hashemite dynasty and played a major role in establishing the modern state of Iraq. During her lifetime, she was highly esteemed and trusted by British officials and given an immense amount of power for a woman of her time. She has been described as 'one of the few representatives of His Majesty's Government remembered by the Arabs with anything resembling affection'.

1. 'The Bell maps have shown the way'

An accurate map denotes a journey
by a man or the woman who traced it.
Its panoramas circumscribed, its grid
locating features, it guides the steps of those
whose role it is to follow.

Her path at first was vague
from where she stood, and who
she was, towards whatever she might be,
the myth she represents.

Breaking bread with tribes,
she crossed conflicted sands.
She spoke their tongue
and understood what lay behind
their words. Surveying skies,
she measured miles.
She haggled for supplies.

And when their land became
their country, she was lionized.

2. Pater
Isaac Lowthian Bell (1816 – 1904)

In that stern, expensive portrait
he may have hung centre stage
just above his mantelpiece,
he is staring back at the world
like a founding father.

Self-contained and righteous,
he is the one who pays
the piper. Like it or not,
for your own good, you'll dance
to the tune he's called.

His name is Isaac Lowthian Bell –
industrial magnate, MP,
and twice elected mayor.
Should any fool forget it, hearken:
he is *Sir* Isaac to you.

His own children and theirs
have always called him 'Pater',
never risking 'Grandpapa'.
Acclaimed by all, his greatness
is planetary, cold, austere.

3. Father and Daughter
Thomas Hugh Bell, (1844 – 1931)

In an emerald green velvet dress
and neat white pinafore against which
her red hair flames, she was a gift
to the artist hired to paint them both.
Hugh's eyes are focused on her,
while she, unconstrained
in his embrace, lets hers wander,
aware that elsewhere
there are parks, ponds, trees.

And who can blame the waywardness
of an eight-year-old tomboy,
cooped up for her sitting
in that airless Victorian room –
respectable, drab and over-furnished?

From each obscure staging post
in far-flung Arabia, she will send
her soothing letters. Newsy, wicked,
full of fun, they'll speak of all the things
he can bear to know.

4. Florence
Florence Bell née *Olliffe (1851 - 1930)*

Quietly manoeuvred into a love match,
Florence was earnest and fitted the bill
for an easy-going widower's wife –
but glamorous, too, and raised in Paris.
Like one who had learned it abroad,
she spoke her native tongue impeccably,
betraying merely a hint of the French
she spoke with ease in salons.

Trying her best to school his children
in the wisdom she adhered to,
she couldn't curb his talented girl,
who read much more than a daughter needs to
and piped up insufferably, goading her
and poor Miss Klug to tears.

5. A Bluestocking

Returning home with a first, cock-a-hoop
and cocky, her 'Oxford ways' perturbed
her family: how would they ever
find her a spouse? At Lady Margaret Hall
Miss Wordsworth had urged
to no avail the role of 'Adam's helpmate'.
Obsessed with 'minor graces',
she had laid claim to reading time
for penmanship and needlework,
or how to open doors discreetly –
lest her charges ruffle
clubbable gents who gawped,
any time her cohort sidled
into lecture halls.
                        She at least,
unconcerned, rose above their scorn
and that of the don who'd wondered:
'What did the ladies make of that?'
when his gist added nothing
to what she'd garnered from his book;
or of one whose facts were wrong:
'I'm sorry', she'd said, 'I disagree'.

6. The Languages She Spoke

Her first tongue was English, handed
down on a silver plate, its vowels
refined through generations
of iron and steel, its range increased
by schooling success had paid for.

Next her governess taught her French
that stepmama had learned in Paris.
She had to speak and write it well:
a lingua franca opening doors
to diplomatic tête-a-têtes.

With German she scaled
the highest peaks, its convolutions
treacherous, its grammar thorny.
Along the way she learned the names
for a swathe of alpine flowers.

In Persian the word for 'paradise'
is intertwined with 'garden', just as soul
and body are in the poetry of Hafiz.
But when she fell in love herself
'adultery' locked the gate.

Gutteral, glottal, and almost
impossible, her Arabic nearly killed her,
yet still she persevered, until her grasp
was perfect, chatting like an equal
in the sumptuous tents of sheiks.

7. The Desert Queen and Lawrence

She addressed him as 'dear boy'. He called her
'Gerty'. Edwardian scholars abroad,
they had both discovered the Arab cause.
Careless of safety, they flouted the rules.

In self-imposed exile they had cut loose
the baggage of gender and class. Branded
a bastard, he was unlikely to rise.
She was a woman who knew her own mind.

Each had taken a first in history.
She had managed hers with a year to spare,
her papers 'delightful'. He was inspired
by desert castles. She had helped on digs.

Until, by chance, nomadic lives began.
Her hat draped in a *keffiyeh*, her skirt
divided, Gertude galloped like a man
in freedom and comfort across the dunes.

A smouldering figure in Bedouin
robes, the prototype for Valentino,
Lawrence appeared to the friends who knew him
undistracted by sexual urges.

He was flamboyant in skirmish and raid.
She homed in on detail. And when she planned
to meet a sheik, her camels were laden
with gifts, pearls and dresses, her canvas bath.

8. Old Maid

How tragic it was or perhaps
a redemption when the decorum
of that age disallowed
her passion
for a man unhappily wed.

Self-assured and strident
in so many ways,
she couldn't face 'adultery'
stretching out between them
like barren sand

across which her letters
trailed until at last
they lay together
in a hopeless
chaste embrace.

Condemned to die *intacta,*
she drew a line
and moved on. Leaving him
to his fate, she was compelled
to accept her own.

9. Mesopotamia, 1921

This is the land
between the rivers:
Uruk, Erech, al-Iraq,
a blighted garden,
a cradle, a zone –
the no-man's-land
disputed
by Sunni, Shia, Kurd;
ruled but
unsubdued
by Ottoman Turks;
a blank canvas,
a mandate
passed on to the Brits –
either *au fait*
and well disposed
like Lawrence,
Bell and Cox
or blimpishly
arrogant, dismissing
the 'Frocks';
and now
for how long
the fiefdom
of Faisal,
established
and sanctioned
by those who count –
where a line
in the sand
is easily drawn,
but just
as soon erased?

10. Iraqi Schoolgirls, 1932

Beyond these walls there's a place
where they are sisters and daughters
and soon, *inshallah*, virtuous
wives- and mothers-to-be.

Out there where modesty's praised,
their future's determined.
Their allurements buried
like a hoard, each bride-price

is settled. Being who they are
and where they come from,
each is a link in the chain
that holds the world together.

The same acquiescence
guarantees their quietness
in this studious room,
where peering eyes absorb

the shapes their fingers follow:
alif, baa, taa ... Filling in
the vowels from memory,
they hear syllables murmuring

inside their heads.
                    And who can say
what they'll make of these things they learn –
their lives safe and circumscribed,
their lips scarcely moving?

AFTER CAVAFY
Όσο μπορείς

Even if your life
is not the one you'd choose
try at least
as best you can
not to demean it
by courting the world
too frantically
with self-serving
moves and chat;
and try not
to cheapen it
by dragging it
here and there
and keeping nothing back
in the daily
exchange
of news and views
with those you think
have made it
until it seems
no more
than a tiresome stranger.

TWO ROOMS
after Van Gogh

1. The Artist's Bedroom

Any room you like can be a refuge –
with three closed walls and a window
through which you glimpse the world.
One by one the walls collapse,
extending your view towards both east
and west, but then revealing everything
you thought you'd left behind. The low
ceiling lifts into a sky so distant
you forget sometimes it's there.

All that remains is a window
that you will slowly fill with bridges,
boats, faces, trees; some yellow, white
or purple flowers; the endless waves
of a cornfield above which a handful
of wind-tossed birds
seem to be holding their own.

2. On the Threshold of Eternity

This is the room where a man sits alone
on a simple chair, his body slumped
in a pose of bleak interrogation,
his tunnel vision to see each work
as a chart of flawed intentions,
his days locked in the bleared lens
of pointless despair, sensing too
beyond the flames of manic summers
that cold stars are turning,
tuned to a shrill monotonous note.

NAVVIES

A blasphemous horde of poachers
and drinkers the big money had spawned,
they dug their way through rocks and sodden clay.
Camped out like tinkers, only their brass
was missed when they picked up sticks,
following the track to another day
of drudgery and dirty looks.

Country lads and migrants,
their mumbles hard to follow –
who thought of them at all
when the band played and folk
clutched tickets for which they had paid?

THRIFT

Through white noise money has made
I hear inherited wisdom. It is battened down
and canny, telling me now to make do and trim,
as if somehow I might succumb
to the unforgiving cycle of extravagance
and meltdown. Stern-voiced, insistent,
it is penny-pinching, penny-wise –
peeking always around the corner.

THE GIRL IN THE PICTURE

The Parthenon behind her,
bleached white in classical light,
is little more than staging,

the backdrop they've chosen
– this girl and the boy who loves her –
to match her flawless style.

And why should a goddess
matter to her, or the distant era
when myths were real?

There are idols enough
for her to aspire to
in the pages of *Vogue* and *Marie Claire*.

The boy is patient and knows
his part: to capture her pose,
when her smile says she's ready.

Her slight form balanced
on elegant, impractical heels,
her head is tilted

to show its more auspicious side.
Between each perfect shot,
she adjusts her hair again.

Brushed out ceremoniously,
it is cast to the wind or rivers
down neck and shoulder.

Oblivious to those
who scurry around her
like so many extras,

she will Instagram her best face
to the friends at home
she keeps updated.

SASSY

Playing cards
at the back of the bus,
Sarah could swear
like one of the boys –
her mouth as foul
as any sailor's.
Scatting hard
across the octaves,
her voice
was like a horn
swapping licks
with bop's elite.
One step ahead
of the changes,
she harnessed time
as if she owned it
in pitch-perfect
glissandos.

THELONIUS

The Baroness Pannonica
his muse, nurse
and patroness,
Nellie also
was his muse
and wife, the mother
of his kids.
Taking the rap
for dope
they'd smoked,
discussing sounds
he'd winkled
from in between the keys,
Nica bailed him
out again.
Holding on
to his cabaret card,
he kept the wolves at bay.

EMPATHY
Seán Ó Ríordáin

'Come across', said Turnbull, 'you will see such sorrow
    in the horse's eyes.
If you had hooves as heavy beneath you, your eyes too
    would be as sad as these.'

And it was clear to me that he sensed so well the sorrow
    in the horse's eyes
and had thought so deeply on it that his own mind in the end
    had drowned in the horse's.

So I looked at the horse to observe the sadness
    deep down in his eyes,
but all I saw was Turnbull staring back towards me
    from the horse's head.

I glanced at Turnbull, then looked at him again
    until I saw in his face
that the great eyes subdued by sorrow
    had now become the horse's.

DETECTIVE

For three nights the yowling
disturbed him, his act of kindness
a bad call when he'd left out
the saucer of milk on his moonlit stoop.

He was tense with work
and a lover's absence. Needing more
than he'd time to spare,
she had handed back his empty hours.

On the afternoon he spent
with the killer something had clicked,
prowling like experts
each other's chosen domain.

There was less than a whisker
between relief and the thrill of doing it.
Staring into the eyes, a pressure builds
too late for it ever to stop.

Couldn't a stray understand
it was just a saucer of milk
with no strings attached;
and she was just some pussy?

PENGUINS ON PARADE
after Willi Ronis

Although they hanker still
for desolate views,
they have learned to count
their blessings: strollers
taking 'a bowl of air'
on this bitter afternoon.

Their formal attire
incongruous, their waddling
gait seems outlandish
to those whose days
they've challenged.

Consorting wisely
with their own,
they have tried at least
to pay their way
and not appear
stand-offish.

With no one else abroad
on walkways,
lawns and benches
you could swear
that they belong,
shaking heads sagely
now that summer's gone.

SEVILLE

As I make it across *Avenida del Cid*
the LED display hits thirty-nine degrees.
Seeking refuge in the Jewish Quarter
I discover a tiled courtyard,
where I sip chill soup they've blended
from oil, tomatoes and a lump
of bread. *Gazpacho*, yes, a revelation
when in such heat I get it.

CHALK
for Edgar Müller

As all worlds are, they're transitory –
those flights of fancy you create
where hurtling waters
tumble down
into a paved surface.

The passers-by are drawn in,
elements, briefly, in a bigger
picture, teetering playfully
on the brink of depths
they cannot fathom.

For who's to say what's real
or where a skewed
perspective takes you,
when sea like a timepiece
returns to desert?

In our cities ambition rises.
The crouching artist
acquires a team. Laying aside
his coloured rocks,
he buys up paint in lots.

So in five days
an ice age happens
or a canal becomes your street.
Dissolving with each downpour,
its waters do not rise.

VENICE

Growing bigger year by year
the cruise ships barely make it.

Bumping along the canal,
their shock waves

judder sunken trees,
unsettling tables and chairs.

One day the deepening water
that's undermined

the basilica's floor
will help to ease their passage …

Chained to rafts painted green,
orange and white

cement mixers
float past serenely.

A ROPE TRICK

Logging the evidence
from travellers' tales,
we learn to live
with rumours,
never knowing for sure
how far opinion
takes us, or whether
a miracle is what
it seems and not
an honest deception.
Staring into the grain
of photos in a book
that has weight
and a feel of its own,
you see how the boy
is balancing
for the price of a meal
where the rope
and the sky
are one.
There are fields
and villages
all around
whose dialects
shift imperceptibly
and mountains
blurred in
shimmering heat.
Look long enough
and you could be him.
Closing your eyes,
there's always
a choice.

FIRE

Like neophytes awaiting the scheduled
mysteries we bring much-travelled voices,
our babble of sterling, dollars, yens –

and if from the start we're almost certain
that the magic is merely sleights,
the ancient play of hoaxers,

still we can't help being drawn
as children are to flames. The rite begins.
The drums are a slow narcosis,

as one adept steps forth
to groom his lucent skin, lingeringly,
in a self-obsessed toilette. Others ingest

forbidden fruit, exhale their fiery word,
or walk unscathed on burning coal
which, when the show is over,

a shadow douses with his bucket,
releasing clouds of damp smoke
and a pungent, cynical hiss.

FOR HOWLIN' WOLF IN HEAVEN

I surf and click, then raise his complex shade,
the presence and the poundage of a man
who took care of business, transcending his name
along the road between White Station,
Mississippi, and the juke joints of Chicago.

A diminutive screen contains him,
as he expounds the meaning of the blues –
a patriarch and mason, who had grasped his letters
like thorns, until his labours found a way
through the entanglement of clauses.

And see him now as he takes the stage
in his ample suit, his ululation rising
from its buried source, a landscape
of estrangement, where his mother
sets her face against his devil's music.

LAKE GARDA

No more than you,
Catullus, do I understand
the violence
that went to make
its calm: the clash
of a planet's
shifting plates
revealing white
escarpments
across a lake
replenished
by glacial streams
until
      crashing down
from the Dolomites,
they're tamed
by milder gods
whose cult
and virtues
you embraced
in friendship,
wit and grace.

MAN ON A WIRE

When he looks back on his life
he will see that the best of it
was a journey he took from A to B
on a wire between two buildings –

his every breath a distillation
of what it meant to keep your nerve
and hold steady, each muscle
braced and quivering like the wire itself

which, at a distance, was no more
than a filament, but close up
was a hawser along which he took
illicit steps, knowing his future

weighed upon them and all things
were simple, once the choice was made,
however the pole teetered
or the air roared wildly

above a world of chairs
and carpets, dates and deliveries,
or the cops who stared amazed
at a man walking across the sky

whom later they cuffed
and cautioned apologetically
before asking him politely his name
and a few relevant details.

ACKNOWLEDGEMENTS

Thanks are due to the editors of the following in which some of these poems or earlier versions of them were first published: *Agenda, Black Sheep Review, Carillon, The Fat Damsel, The Galway Review, The Grey Suit Poetry Stream, The Jazz Centre (UK) Newsletter, The Journal, Message in a Bottle, New Walk, The Ofi Press Magazine, Old Belongings* (Reading University Creative Arts Anthology 2015), *Versions of the North, Your one Phone Call, Pennine Platform, Poets in Person* (edited by Aprilia Zank for Indigo Dreams Publishing 2014), and *Yareah* (USA). I am also grateful to Susan Jeffers, whose 'self help' book, *Feel the Fear and Do it Anyway*, gave me the idea for my opening villanelle. Note: On page 60, 'a bowl of air' is a literal translation of the French phrase: *un bol d'air* meaning 'a breath of fresh air'.

ABOUT THE AUTHOR

David Cooke was born in the UK in 1953 to a family that comes from the West of Ireland. He won a Gregory Award in 1977, while still an undergraduate at Nottingham University. After publishing his first full poetry collection in 1984, he then wrote no poetry for two decades, during which time he was Head of Modern Languages in a large comprehensive school in Cleethorpes. Subsequently, he earned his living as an online bookseller, but is now happily retired and living in Swindon. He is married with four grown-up children.